Gleich · Reindl · Schmidt · Schöpe

Ferienheft
Englisch

Fit ins neue Schuljahr

4

Volksschule

VERITAS
Gemeinsam besser lernen

1. Fill in.

My name is
Helen.

2. Number in the correct order.

3. What do they say? Write.

Good night.
Good afternoon.
Good evening.
Good morning.

1. Find the words and draw lines.

Finde die Wörter und kreise sie ein. Verbinde dann mit dem richtigen Bild.

2. What's Sally's favourite colour? Do the crossword.

Finde Sallys Lieblingsfarbe heraus.

grey
yellow
blue
green
pink

My favourite colour is blue.

Verbinde mit den richtigen Farben. Achtung, zu zwei Bildern gehören mehrere Farben.

3. Draw lines.

grey
blue
black
green
red
brown
yellow

4. Write and colour.

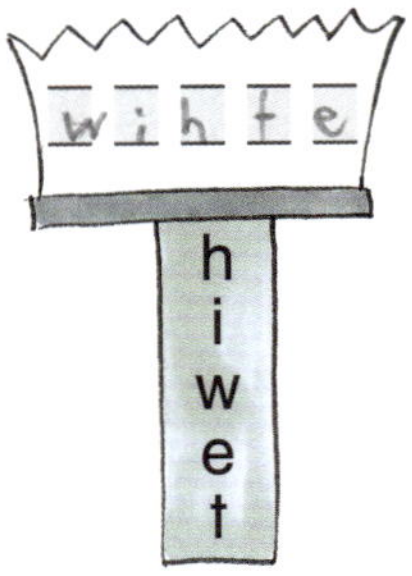

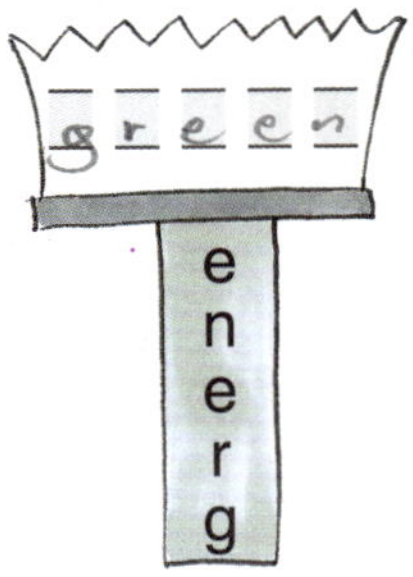

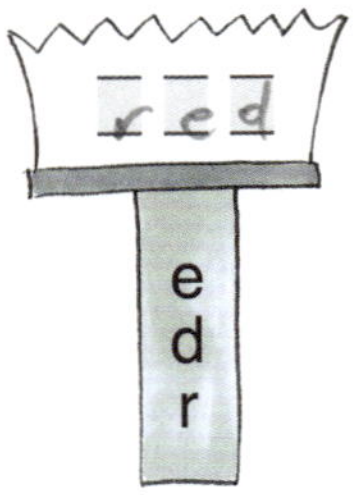

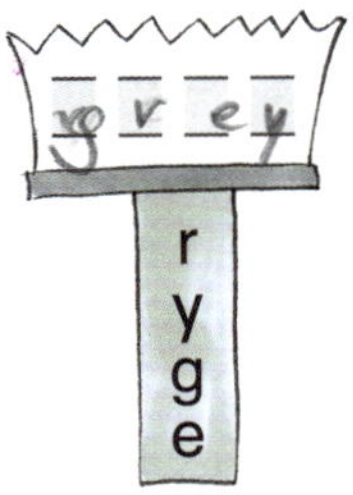

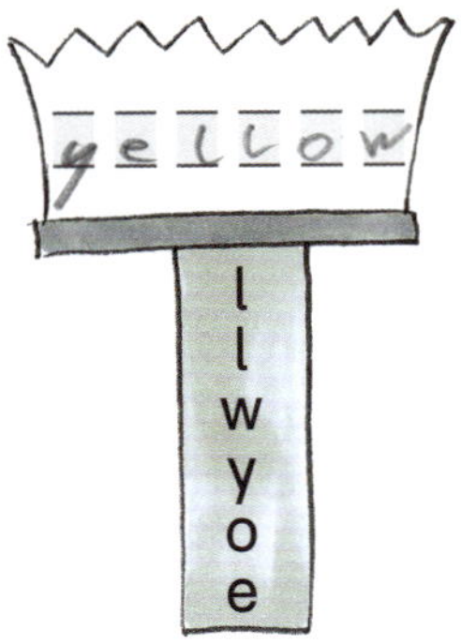

yellow
green
white
red
purple
grey

Was soll das denn heißen?

Da sind Buchstaben durcheinandergekommen. Schreibe erst das Wort, male dann den Pinsel in der richtigen Farbe an.

5. Find the words and circle them.

y	m	a	b	j	l	g
e	o	g	r	e	e	n
l	r	g	o	h	b	h
l	a	e	w	d	l	a
o	n	a	n	v	u	u
w	g	a	g	r	e	y
r	e	d	c	u	k	p
f	g	n	i	z	h	u
o	b	w	h	i	t	e

orange	brown
green	yellow
red	white
grey	blue

6. What colour is missing? Write.

red + blue = ~~grey~~ Porppel

yellow + blue = green

yellow + grenn = orange

black + white = grey

1. Write the numbers in the correct order.

one

2. Count and write.

3. Do you know the word? Write.

nine → ________

five → ________

seven → ________

one → ________

eight → ________

ten → ________

4. How many lollies? Trace the lines and write.

 ________ lollies

 ________ lollies

 ________ lollies

 ________ lollies

5. How much is it? Write.

three + one = ____________ ten – seven = ____________

two + five = ____________ five – four = ____________

three + six = ____________ seven – five = ____________

four + one = ____________ nine – eight = ____________

6. Correct or wrong? Tick.

	correct	wrong
There are **two** .	◯	◯
There is **one** .	◯	◯
There are **eight** .	◯	◯
There are **seven** .	◯	◯

1. Number.

1 schoolbag
2 book
3 folder
4 ruler
5 pencil case
6 pencil
7 rubber
8 scissors
9 glue

2. Draw lines.

lollipop lady
board
teacher
chalk
desk
pen
picture
poster
computer

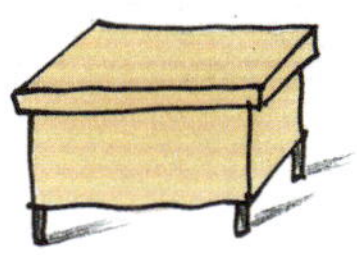

3. Odd one out.

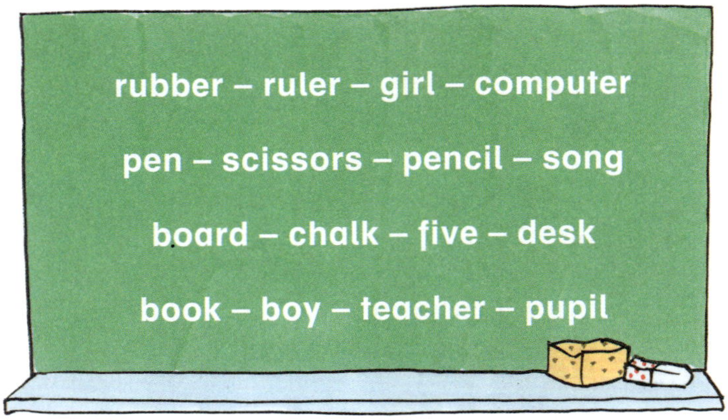

4. Read, look and write. What's missing?

What's missing on Steve's desk?

The ______________ is missing.

What's missing on Kathy's desk?

The ______________ is missing.

What's missing on Polly's desk?

The ______________ is missing.

5. Read and colour.

The pencil case is green.

The ruler is yellow.

The pen is red.

The pencil is blue.

The rubber is pink.

The lollipop is purple.

6. What belongs into the schoolbag? Write.

pencil ruler
scissors pencil case
desk chalk board
poster folder
pen glue rubber
computer book

Finde die Wörter senkrecht und waagrecht. Kreise sie ein. Trage sie dann unten richtig ein.

1. Find the words and circle them. Fill in.

n	b	o	d	y	t	u	r	z	l	u	q
s	h	a	n	d	s	x	c	b	e	l	v
f	a	w	a	r	m	s	p	y	g	m	h
e	s	q	r	b	m	l	o	p	s	y	a
e	c	v	e	f	o	o	t	a	b	u	i
t	h	y	b	t	j	k	h	w	e	f	r
z	e	h	l	a	e	y	e	s	k	l	p
w	a	y	f	i	n	g	e	r	s	c	n
b	d	m	n	q	r	u	h	l	p	q	o
w	d	g	h	m	m	o	u	t	h	y	s
d	e	a	r	s	g	t	o	e	s	y	e
g	h	a	k	n	e	e	s	l	o	p	g

body	**hair**
foot	**ears**
feet	**toes**
head	**hands**
legs	**nose**
arms	**mouth**
eyes	**knees**
fingers	

I've got 2 ______________  .

I've got 2 ______________  and 10 ______________ 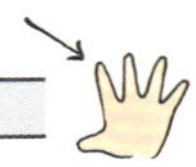 .

I see with my ______________  .

I hear with my ______________  .

I smell with my ______________  .

I speak with my ______________  .

I've got 2 ______________  and 2 ______________ 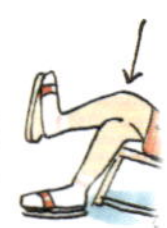 .

This is 1 ______________  and these are 2 ______________ 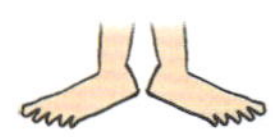

And I've got 10 ______________ 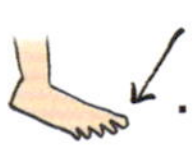 .

2. How do they feel? Draw lines and write.

How do you feel, Jack?

I'm ______________ .

I want to eat a sandwich.

How do you feel, Susan?

I'm ______________ .

It's my birthday.

How do you feel, Sam?

I'm ______________ .

I don't like spiders.

happy

sad

hungry

angry

scared

tired

fine

How do you feel, Jim?

I'm ______________ .

I broke my arm.

How do you feel, Annie?

I'm ______________ .

I can't watch TV.

How do you feel, Maggie?

I'm ______________ .

I want to go to bed.

How do you feel, Liz?

I'm ______________ , thank you.

3. Which alien is it? Read and number.

Alien number one has got two heads, five legs and three arms. It's happy.

Alien number two has got two heads, two noses and one big ear. It's angry.

Alien number three has got one head, four eyes and one mouth with two teeth.

Alien number four has got one head, five feet, one ear and one arm.

Alien number five has got ________ arms, ________ legs, ________ fingers and ________ noses.

1. What is it? Draw lines and write.

teddy bear

castle

inline skates

lorry

racing car

computer game

doll

helicopter

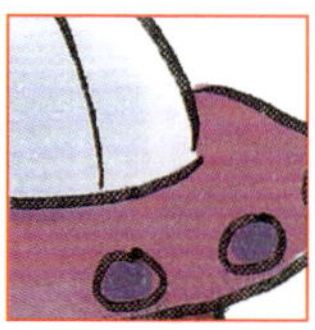

ball

spaceship

2. Do the crossword.

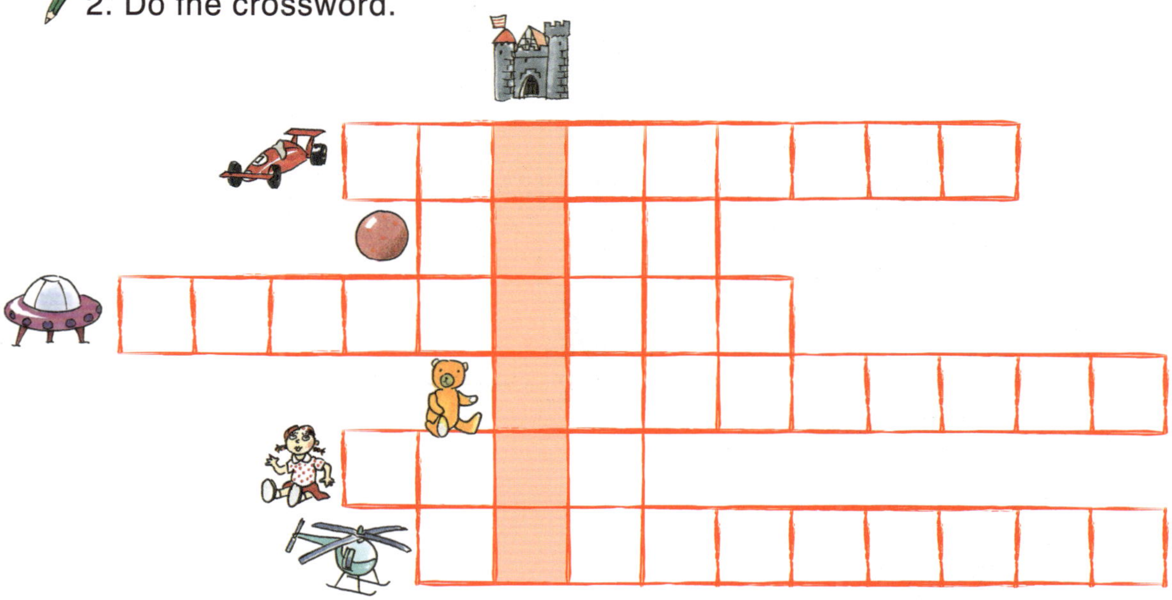

3. At the toy shop.
Match the pictures to the speech bubbles. Draw lines and fill in.

It's ______________ £.

Hello, can I help you?

Thank you. Goodbye.

I like this ______________________.
How much is it?

4. Trace the lines and write.

Katie buys a ______________________ . It's __________ £.

Ken buys a ______________________ . It's __________ £.

Anne buys a ______________________ . It's __________ £.

Derek buys a ______________________ . It's __________ £.

Betty buys a ______________________ . It's __________ £.

racing car **teddy bear** **helicopter** **doll** **spaceship**

1. Such a long scarf! Find the words. Draw lines and write.

__________, __________, __________,

__________, __________, __________,

__________ This word is missing: __________

2. Look and write.

Jenny puts on her __________ ,

her __________ 

and her __________ .

Brian takes off his __________ , his

__________ 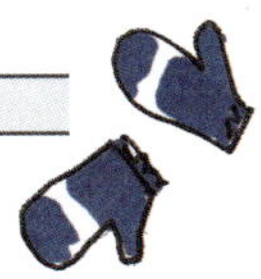 and his __________ .

shoes	**gloves**	**scarf**	**dress**	**woolly hat**	**anorak**

3. What can you see? Write.

shoes – a pullover –
a skirt – a jacket

a pair of trousers –
a pullover –
a T-shirt – a dress

a pair of shorts –
socks – a T-shirt –
a pullover

4. Dress Janet and Jack. Write.

Janet: ______________________________

____

Jack: ______________________________

____

5. Funny  . Read and tick.

It's wearing…

- ◯ a woolly hat, a jacket, a pair of trousers and shoes.
- ◯ a cap, a scarf, a jacket, a pair of shorts and boots.
- ◯ a cap, a scarf, an anorak, a pair of trousers and shoes.

It's wearing…

- ◯ a woolly hat, a pullover, a pair of trousers and gloves.
- ◯ a cap, an anorak, a T-shirt, a pair of shorts and boots.
- ◯ a jacket, a woolly hat, socks, a pair of trousers and shoes.

It's wearing…

- ◯ gloves, a woolly hat, a shirt, a skirt and boots.
- ◯ gloves, a scarf, a woolly hat, a pullover and a pair of trousers.
- ◯ a T-shirt, a dress, a cap, a pair of shorts and shoes.

1. Look outside the windows. What's the weather like? Write.

It's ______________ .

It's ______________

and ______________ .

snowy
hot
foggy
rainy
sunny
windy
cloudy
cold

It's ______________

and ______________ .

It's ______________

and ______________

and ______________ .

2. Odd one out.

snowy – cold – hot

sunny – cloudy – rainy

sunny – hot – snowy

windy – hot – rainy

3. Fill in the missing letters. Draw lines and write.

1. _onday
2. _uesday
3. Wednes___
4. Thursday
5. _riday
6. _atur___
7. Su_day

On Monday it's sunny.

On ________ it's ________.

On ________ it's ________.

________________________________.

________________________________.

________________________________.

On ________ it's ________

and ________.

Thursday Monday Friday Tuesday Saturday Wednesday
Sunday sunny rainy (2x) foggy windy snowy cloudy (2x)

LÖSUNGEN

4

VERITAS

Gemeinsam besser lernen

VERITAS
Gemeinsam besser lernen

Gemeinsam besser lernen mit …

Ferienhefte für die Volksschule:

Natürlich sind die **Ferien** in erster Linie zur Erholung da. Ein paar Tage vor Beginn des neuen Schuljahres können viele Kinder aber doch einige Minuten täglich für die **Vorbereitung nutzen**. In unseren **Ferienheften** sind die wichtigsten Kapitel eines Schuljahres in **überschaubaren Portionen** zusammengefasst und ermöglichen so ein **effizientes Lernen**. Das Bearbeiten der Aufgaben macht richtig Spaß, denn die Inhalte sind sehr abwechslungsreich und spielerisch aufbereitet.

Die ideale Ferienkost:

- abwechslungsreiche Übungen sorgen (auch bei Schlechtwetter) für viel Spaß
- Wiederholungen des (Vor-)Jahresstoffes in überschaubaren Portionen
- inkl. Lösungen (zur Selbstkontrolle)
- auch für Auto- und Bahnfahrten geeignet

Ferienheft Deutsch 4. Volksschule

Fit ins neue Schuljahr

Catherine Salomon, Jutta Schabhüttl

32 Seiten, 19 x 26 cm, 4-färbig,
inkl. Lösungsheft
ISBN 978-3-7101-0377-3

Ferienheft Lesen 4. Volksschule

Fit ins neue Schuljahr

Cornelia Scholtes, Ursula von Kuester, Annette Webersberger

48 Seiten, 19 x 26 cm, 4-färbig,
inkl. Lösungsheft
ISBN 978-3-7101-0380-3

Zahlenreise 4. Ferienheft

Zur Vorbereitung auf die 5. Schulstufe

Catherine Salomon, Jutta Schabhüttl

48 Seiten, 19 x 26 cm, 4-färbig,
inkl. Lösungsheft
ISBN 978-3-7058-8240-9

Erhältlich direkt beim Verlag oder bei Ihrem Buchhändler

Bestellen Sie online, rufen Sie an oder schicken Sie ein Fax oder E-Mail:
Tel.: +43 732 776451-2280 · Fax: +43 732 776451-2239 · E-Mail: kundenberatung@veritas.at

www.veritas.at

(Zum Herausnehmen dieses Lösungsheftes die mittlere Klammer lösen.)

Informationen für Eltern und Lehrkräfte

Englisch spielerisch üben mit dem Englisch Ferienheft

Das Englisch-Sprachniveau, auf dem sich SchülerInnen am Ende der Volksschule befinden ist sehr unterschiedlich. Mit diesem Ferienheft üben und sichern die Kinder auf spielerische Weise den für den Schulübertritt wichtigen Wortschatz sowie ihr Lese- und Schreibvermögen. Abwechslungsreiche Übungsformen und ansprechende Illustrationen motivieren, Wörter und Strukturen vielfältig anzuwenden.

Das Känguru Sally ist dabei ständiger Begleiter. Die Kinder Lisa und Max geben Tipps und Hilfestellung in deutscher Sprache. Eindeutige Aufgabenstellungen und Selbstkontrolle durch den Lösungsteil ermöglichen den Kindern, eigenständig mit dem Englisch Ferienheft zu arbeiten.

In 15 leicht verdaulichen Tagesportionen werden verschiedene Themenbereiche behandelt, jede Menge Rätselspaß inklusive. Als besonderen Anreiz dürfen sich die Kinder nach jedem Thema mit einem Puzzleteil belohnen, das sie von der letzten Seite des Buches ausschneiden und auf den hinteren Innenumschlag kleben. Dies ergibt schließlich ein schönes Gesamtbild.

Das Englisch Ferienheft Volksschule unterstützt die spielerische Auseinandersetzung mit Englisch und fördert die Freude am Erlernen der Fremdsprache. Ganz nebenbei dient es aber auch einem …

… entspannten Englisch-Start – in der weiterführenden Schule!

Achtung: Alle Lösungen sind hier mit roter Schrift eingetragen.

Inhalt

Hello — Tag 1

1. Fill in.

2. Number in the correct order.

3

Schreibe in die richtigen Sprechblasen.

3. What do they say? Write.

Good night.
Good afternoon.
Good evening.
Good morning.

1. Find the words and draw lines.

Finde die Wörter und kreise sie ein. Verbinde dann mit dem richtigen Bild.

2. What's Sally's favourite colour? Do the crossword.

			P	I	N	K
	B	L	U	E		
		G	R	E	E	N
			P			
Y	E	L	L	O	W	
	G	R	E	Y		

Finde Sallys Lieblingsfarbe heraus.

grey
yellow
blue
green
pink

My favourite colour is purple.

3. Draw lines.

Verbinde mit den richtigen Farben. Achtung, zu zwei Bildern gehören mehrere Farben.

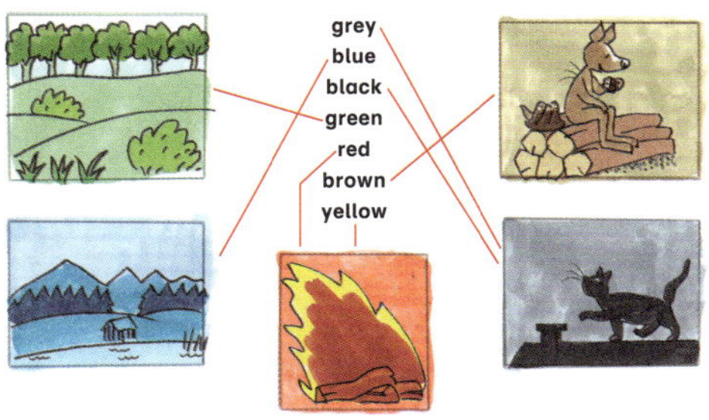

4. Write and colour.

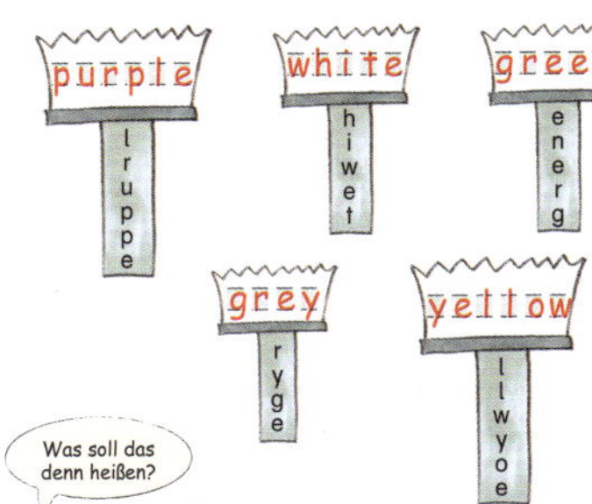

yellow
green
white
red
purple
grey

5. Find the words and circle them.

Suche die Wörter senkrecht und waagrecht. Kreise ein.

y	m	a	b	j	l	g
e	o	g	r	e	e	n
l	r	g	o	h	b	h
l	a	e	w	d	l	a
o	n	a	n	v	u	u
w	g	a	g	r	e	y
r	e	d	c	u	k	p
f	g	n	i	z	h	u
o	b	w	h	i	t	e

orange
green
red
grey

brown
yellow
white
blue

6. What colour is missing? Write.

Welche Farben fehlen? Schreibe die Wörter in der richtigen Farbe dazu.

red + blue = purple

yellow + blue = green

yellow + red = orange

black + white = grey

1. Write the numbers in the correct order.

one, two, three, four,
five, six, seven, eight,
nine, ten

2. Count and write.

eight three five six

3. Do you know the word? Write.

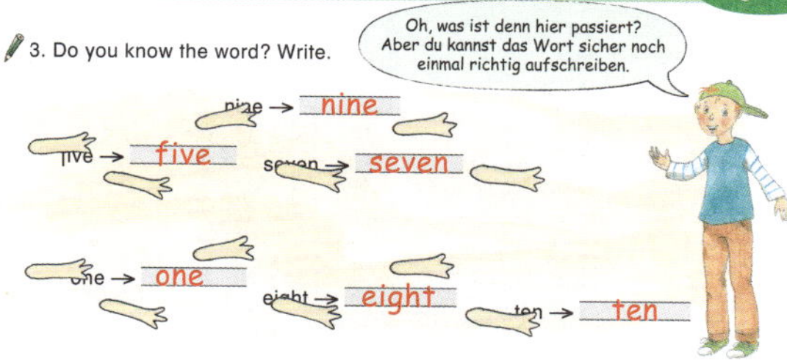

nine → nine
five → five
seven → seven
one → one
eight → eight
ten → ten

4. How many lollies? Trace the lines and write.

ten lollies
four lollies
six lollies
eight lollies

5. How much is it? Write.

three + one = four
two + five = seven
three + six = nine
four + one = five
ten – seven = three
five – four = one
seven – five = two
nine – eight = one

6. Correct or wrong? Tick.

	correct	wrong
There are **two** (ladybird).	✓	
There is **one** (dragonfly).		✓
There are **eight** (butterfly).		✓
There are **seven** (bee).	✓	

1. Number.

1 schoolbag
2 book
3 folder
4 ruler
5 pencil case
6 pencil
7 rubber
8 scissors
9 glue

2. Draw lines.

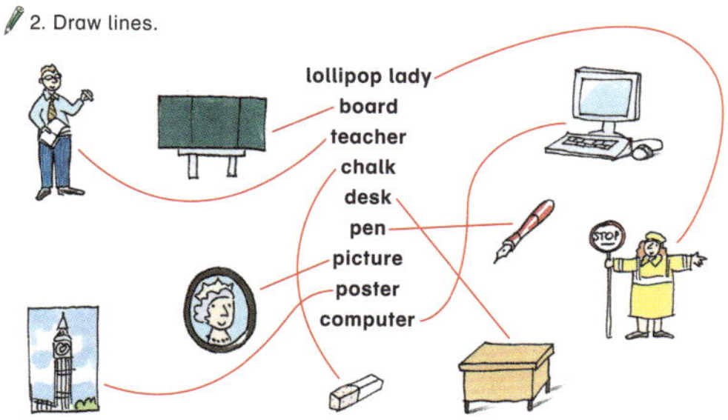

3. Odd one out.

rubber – ruler – ~~girl~~ – computer
pen – scissors – pencil – ~~song~~
board – chalk – ~~five~~ – desk
~~book~~ – boy – teacher – pupil

4. Read, look and write. What's missing?

What's missing on Steve's desk?
The pencil is missing.

What's missing on Kathy's desk?
The rubber is missing.

What's missing on Polly's desk?
The folder is missing.

5. Read and colour.

The pencil case is green.
The ruler is yellow.
The pen is red.
The pencil is blue.
The rubber is pink.
The lollipop is purple.

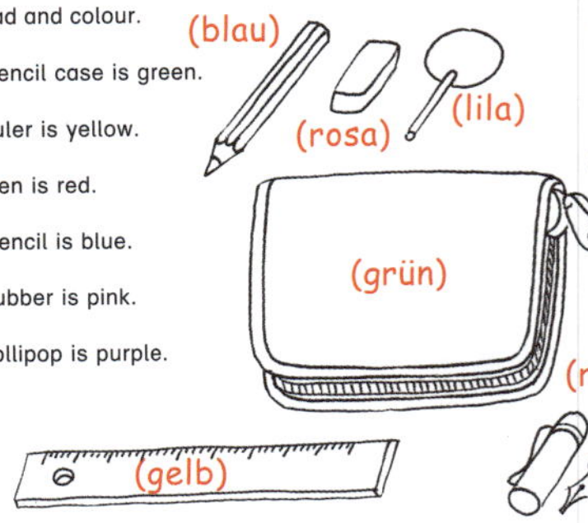

6. What belongs into the schoolbag? Write.

pencil, ruler, scissors, pencil case, desk, chalk, board, poster, folder, pen, glue, rubber, computer, book

book, folder, glue, pen, pencil,
pencil case, rubber, ruler,
scissors

1. Find the words and circle them. Fill in.

n	b	o	d	y	t	u	r	z	l	u	q
s	h	a	n	d	s	x	c	b	e	l	v
f	a	w	a	r	m	s	p	y	g	m	h
e	s	q	r	b	m	l	o	p	s	y	a
e	c	v	e	f	o	o	t	a	b	u	i
t	h	y	b	t	j	k	h	w	e	f	r
z	e	h	l	a	e	y	e	s	k	l	p
w	a	y	f	i	n	g	e	r	s	c	n
b	d	m	n	q	r	u	h	l	p	q	o
w	d	g	h	m	m	o	u	t	h	y	s
d	e	a	r	s	g	t	o	e	s	y	e
g	h	a	k	n	e	e	s	l	o	p	g

body	hair
foot	ears
feet	toes
head	hands
legs	nose
arms	mouth
eyes	knees
fingers	

I've got 2 arms.
I've got 2 hands and 10 fingers.
I see with my eyes.
I hear with my ears.
I smell with my nose.
I speak with my mouth.
I've got 2 legs and 2 knees.
This is 1 foot and these are 2 feet.
And I've got 10 toes.

2. How do they feel? Draw lines and write.

happy – sad – hungry – angry – scared – tired – fine

How do you feel, Jack?
I'm hungry.
I want to eat a sandwich.

How do you feel, Jim?
I'm sad.
I broke my arm.

How do you feel, Susan?
I'm happy.
It's my birthday.

How do you feel, Annie?
I'm angry.
I can't watch TV.

How do you feel, Sam?
I'm scared.
I don't like spiders.

How do you feel, Maggie?
I'm tired.
I want to go to bed.

How do you feel, Liz?
I'm fine, thank you.

3. Which alien is it? Read and number.

Alien number one has got two heads, five legs and three arms.
It's happy.

Alien number two has got two heads, two noses and one big ear.
It's angry.

Alien number three has got one head, four eyes and one mouth with two teeth.

Alien number four has got one head, five feet, one ear and one arm.

Alien number five has got four arms, three legs, four fingers and two noses.

1. What is it? Draw lines and write.

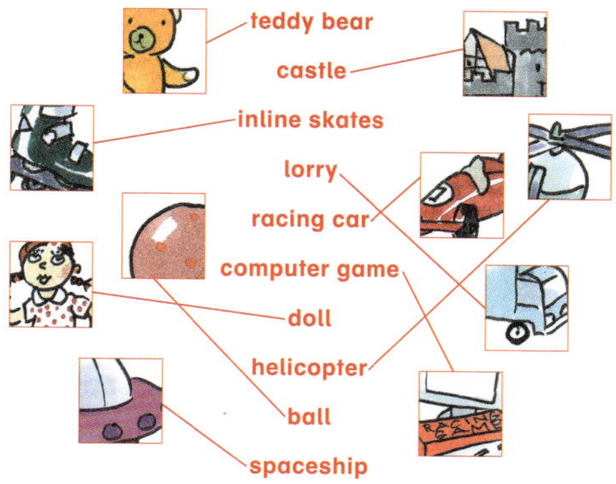

2. Do the crossword.

3. At the toy shop.
Match the pictures to the speech bubbles. Draw lines and fill in.

4. Trace the lines and write.

Katie buys a doll. It's 4 (four) £.

Ken buys a racing car. It's 8 (eight) £.

Anne buys a spaceship. It's 6 (six) £.

Derek buys a helicopter. It's 10 (ten) £.

Betty buys a teddy bear. It's 5 (five) £.

racing car teddy bear helicopter doll spaceship

1. Such a long scarf! Find the words. Draw lines and write.

skirt, trousers, pullover,
boots, cap, socks,
shirt This word is missing: T-shirt

2. Look and write.

Jenny puts on her dress, her anorak and her shoes.
Brian takes off his woolly hat, his gloves and his scarf.

shoes gloves scarf dress woolly hat anorak

3. What can you see? Write.

shoes – a pullover – **a skirt** – **a jacket**

a pair of trousers – **a pullover** – a T-shirt – **a dress**

a pair of shorts – **socks** – **a T-shirt** – a pullover

4. Dress Janet and Jack. Write.

(mögliche Lösung)

Janet: a skirt, a T-Shirt, socks, (pink) shoes, a woolly hat, a scarf, a jacket

Jack: a pair of trousers, a shirt, gloves, a cap, a pullover, (brown) shoes, an anorak, socks

5. Funny [picture]. Read and tick.

It's wearing…
- ○ a woolly hat, a jacket, a pair of trousers and shoes.
- ✓ a cap, a scarf, a jacket, a pair of shorts and boots.
- ○ a cap, a scarf, an anorak, a pair of trousers and shoes.

It's wearing…
- ○ a woolly hat, a pullover, a pair of trousers and gloves.
- ○ a cap, an anorak, a T-shirt, a pair of shorts and boots.
- ✓ a jacket, a woolly hat, socks, a pair of trousers and shoes.

It's wearing…
- ✓ gloves, a woolly hat, a shirt, a skirt and boots.
- ○ gloves, a scarf, a woolly hat, a pullover and a pair of trousers.
- ○ a T-shirt, a dress, a cap, a pair of shorts and shoes.

1. Look outside the windows. What's the weather like? Write.

It's foggy.

It's sunny and hot.

snowy hot foggy rainy sunny windy cloudy cold

It's snowy and cold.

It's cloudy and windy and rainy.

2. Odd one out.

snowy – cold – ~~hot~~

~~sunny~~ – cloudy – rainy

sunny – hot – ~~snowy~~

windy – ~~hot~~ – rainy

3. Fill in the missing letters. Draw lines and write.

1. Monday
2. Tuesday
3. Wednesday
4. Thursday
5. Friday
6. Saturday
7. Sunday

On Monday it's sunny.
On Tuesday it's foggy.
On Wednesday it's windy.
On Thursday it's snowy.
On Friday it's rainy.
On Saturday it's cloudy.
On Sunday it's cloudy and rainy.

Thursday	Monday	Friday	Tuesday	Saturday	Wednesday
Sunday	sunny	rainy (2x)	foggy	windy	snowy cloudy (2x)

4. Read the comic.

Crazy weather

1. Draw lines and write.

mother, sister, brother, father,
grandmother, grandfather

2. Look and write.

grandpa
grandma
mum
dad

3. Find the words and write. Then solve the riddles.

Mike's family tree

He's my mum's dad.
He's my grandpa.

She's my dad's sister.
She's my aunt.

She's my dad's mum.
She's my grandma.

He's my mum's brother.
He's my uncle.

4. Read and write.

My best friend has got long brown hair. She is wearing a pink pullover.

My best friend is Lucy.

My best friend is a boy. He has got short blond hair and is wearing a pair of grey shorts.

My best friend is Ben.

My best friend has got brown hair. She likes her inline skates very much.

My best friend is Anna.

My best friend is wearing a blue T-shirt. He has got black hair.

My best friend is John.

5. An interview. Read and fill in.

my brother Joe and my brother Tom

my sister Helen

my friend David

Sam, 9 years

: Hello. What's your name?

: My name is Sam.

: How old are you?

: I'm nine years old.

: Have you got brothers?

: Yes. I have got two brothers, Joe and Tom.

: And how many sisters have you got?

: I have got one sister. Her name is Helen.

: Who is your best friend?

: My best friend is David.

1. Number and write.

- 3 hot chocolate
- 8 coffee
- 2 tea
- 9 orange juice
- 4 milk
- 6 coke
- 5 lemonade
- 1 water
- 7 apple juice

2. Look at the pictures. Find the words and circle them. What's missing?

This word is missing: orange juice

3. Look and write.

My favourite drink is coke.

My favourite drink is lemonade.

My favourite drink is coffee.

My favourite drink is milk.

My favourite drink is water.

My favourite drink is tea.

My favourite drink is orange juice.

My favourite drink is apple juice.

My favourite drink is hot chocolate.

hot chocolate coffee tea orange juice milk coke lemonade water apple juice

1. Look and write.

cornflakes honey bacon egg jam roll butter bread toast ham

2. Find the words and write.

r … ll — roll

b … n — bacon

e … — egg

corn … s — cornflakes

ho … y — honey

3. Read and draw lines.

4. What's missing? Read and draw.

5. Read and number.

I don't like cornflakes, but I like coffee. (2)

I like toast, but I don't like hot chocolate. (3)

I don't like toast. (1)

I don't like ham. (4)

6. Crazy breakfast. What's wrong? Write.

Irgendwie sind die Sätze durcheinandergeraten. Schreibe sie richtig auf.

I like a roll with tea and a cup of jam.
I like a roll with jam and a cup of tea.

I like toast with cornflakes and honey with milk.
I like toast with honey and cornflakes with milk.

I like bread with orange juice and a glass of ham.
I like bread with ham and a glass of orange juice.

1. Do the crossword.

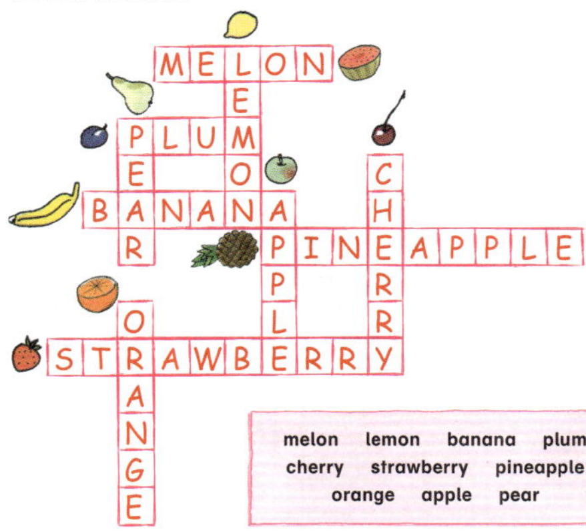

melon lemon banana plum cherry strawberry pineapple orange apple pear

2. Find the fruit in the basket. Write.

banana

lemon

melon

pear

pineapple

3. Trace the lines and write.

Dave likes plums.

Sarah likes strawberries.

Emily likes oranges.

Tim likes apples.

Mary likes cherries.

strawberries cherries apples plums oranges

4. Guess the fruit and write.

5. Read the comic.

Yummy fruit juices

1. What pet is it? Write and draw lines.

budgie cat dog fish guinea pig hamster mouse rabbit tortoise

My pet is red. It can swim.
It's a fish.

My pet is black. It says "miaow".
It's a cat.

My pet is blue. It can fly.
It's a budgie.

My pet is brown and white. It's very small.
It's a hamster.

My pet is brown. It says "bow-wow".
It's a dog.

My pet is black and white. It likes apples.
It's a guinea pig.

My pet is green. It has got short legs.
It's a tortoise.

My pet is white. It has got long ears.
It's a rabbit.

2. Find the pets and colour the fields green. What can you see?

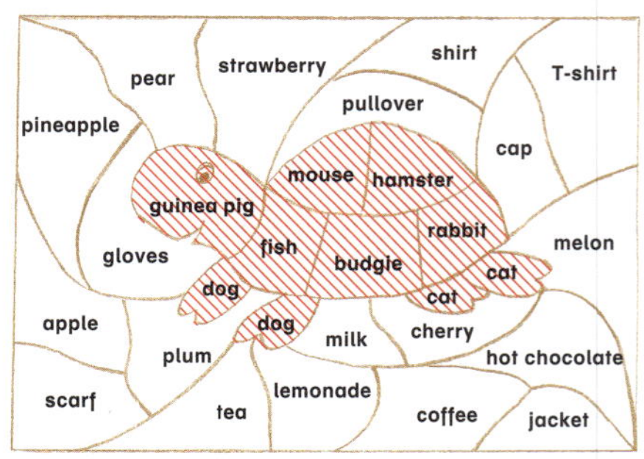

I can see a tortoise.

3. Guess the pets. Write.

rabbit, cat, mouse, dog

4. Trace the lines and write.

A dog likes (ham).
A cat likes (fish).
A rabbit likes (carrots).
A guinea pig likes (apples).
A mouse likes (cheese).

mouse
cat
guinea pig
dog
rabbit

1. Write and draw lines.

spring	summer
autumn	winter

It's spring. (May, April, March)

It's summer. (June, August, July)

It's autumn. (September, November, October)

It's winter. (January, February, December)

2. Write the 12 months in the correct order.

1. January 2. February 3. March
4. April 5. May 6. June
7. July 8. August 9. September
10. October 11. November 12. December

3. Read and tick the correct answer.

Easter is in ...
- winter
- summer
- ✓ spring.

Christmas is in ...
- ✓ December
- November
- September.

Halloween is in ...
- April
- ✓ October
- February.

The summer holidays are in ...
- January
- March
- ✓ July/August.

4. What can you see? Write.

pond
butter-fly
tree
grass
frog
flower

I can see a tree.

I can see a flower.

I can see a frog.

I can see a pond.

I can see grass.

I can see a butterfly.

5. Find the months. Draw lines and write.

Octo- Novem- Jul- Janua- Mar- -ber Decem- Septem-

September, October, November, December

6. What can you see?
Colour the spring words green, the summer words yellow, the autumn words brown and the winter words blue.

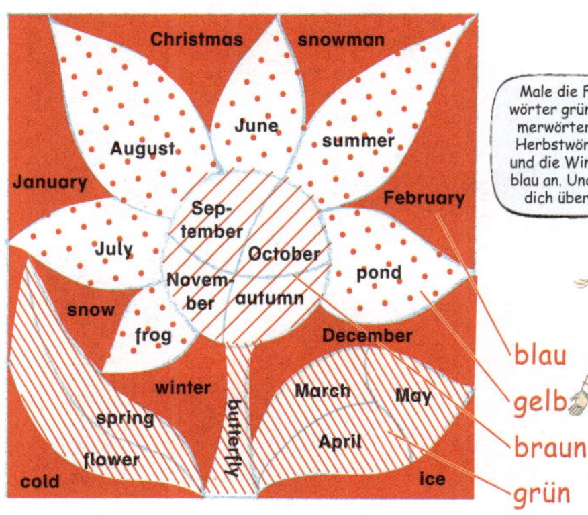

I can see a flower.

1. Read the comic.

Sally in London

2. Colour the British flag – The Union Jack.

3. What can you see in the pictures? Write.

Tower Bridge

London Eye

Buckingham Palace

Big Ben

Buckingham Palace	Tower Bridge	London Eye	Big Ben

4. Read the comic.

Crazy weather

1. Draw lines and write.

mother

sister

brother

father

grandmother

grandfather

2. Look and write.

grandpa
grandma
mum
dad

3. Find the words and write. Then solve the riddles.

Mike's family tree

He's my mum's dad.
He's my grandpa.

She's my dad's mum.
She's my ______.

She's my dad's sister.
She's my ______.

He's my mum's brother.
He's my ______.

4. Read and write.

My best friend has got long brown hair. She is wearing a pink pullover.

My best friend is ______________ .

My best friend is a boy. He has got short blond hair and is wearing a pair of grey shorts.

My best friend is ______________ .

My best friend has got brown hair. She likes her inline skates very much.

My best friend is ______________ .

My best friend is wearing a blue T-shirt.
He has got black hair.

My best friend is ______________ .

5. An interview. Read and fill in.

my brother Joe and my brother Tom

my sister Helen

my friend David

Sam, 9 years

: Hello. What's your name?

: My name is ______________ .

: How old are you?

: I'm ______________ years old.

: Have you got brothers?

: Yes. I have got ______________ , Joe and Tom.

: And how many sisters have you got?

: I have got ______________ . Her name is ______________ .

: Who is your best friend?

: My best ______________ is ______________ .

1. Number and write.

- ◯ hot chocolate
- ◯ coffee
- ◯ tea
- ◯ orange juice
- ◯ milk
- ◯ coke
- ◯ lemonade
- ◯ water
- ◯ apple juice

2. Look at the pictures. Find the words and circle them. What's missing?

This word is missing: ____________________

3. Look and write.

My favourite drink
is ____________ .

My favourite drink
is ____________ .

My favourite drink
is ____________ .

My favourite drink
is ____________ .

My favourite drink
is ____________ .

My favourite drink
is ____________ .

My favourite drink
is ____________
____________ .

My favourite drink
is ____________
____________ .

My favourite drink
is ____________
____________ .

hot chocolate   coffee   tea   orange juice   milk
coke   lemonade   water   apple juice

1. Look and write.

cornflakes honey bacon egg jam roll butter bread toast ham

2. Find the words and write.

r  ll

b  n

e 

corn  s

ho  y

3. Read and draw lines.

4. What's missing? Read and draw.

5. Read and number.

 I don't like cornflakes, but I like coffee. ◯

 I like toast, but I don't like hot chocolate. ◯

 I don't like toast. ◯

 I don't like ham. ◯

6. Crazy breakfast. What's wrong? Write.

 I like a roll with tea and a cup of jam.

____

 I like toast with cornflakes and honey with milk.

____

 I like bread with orange juice and a glass of ham.

____

1. Do the crossword.

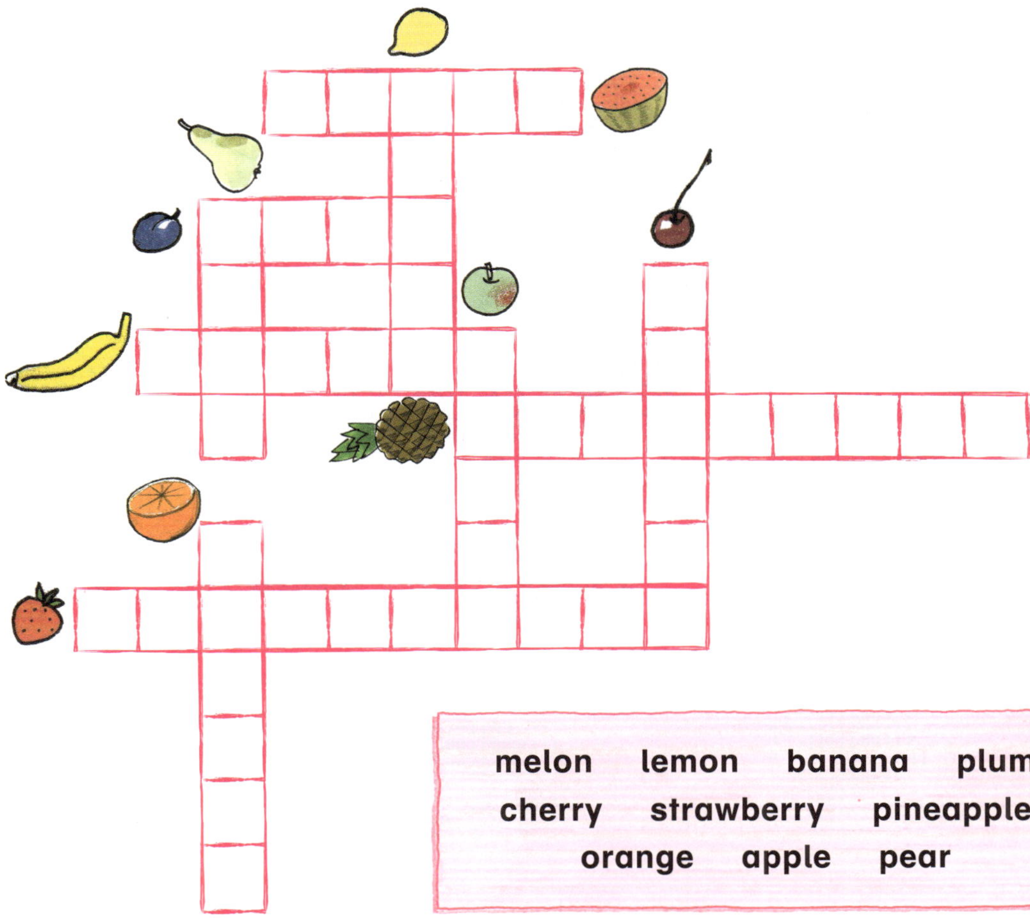

melon lemon banana plum
cherry strawberry pineapple
orange apple pear

2. Find the fruit in the basket. Write.

3. Trace the lines and write.

__________ likes plums.

__________ likes __________ .

__________ likes __________ .

__________ likes __________ .

__________ likes __________ .

strawberries cherries apples plums oranges

4. Guess the fruit and write.

banana
pear
melon
apple

5. Read the comic.

Yummy fruit juices

1. What pet is it? Write and draw lines.

budgie	cat
dog	fish
guinea pig	
hamster	mouse
rabbit	tortoise

My pet is red. It can swim.
It's a ______________ .

My pet is black. It says "miaow".
It's a ______________ .

My pet is blue. It can fly.
It's a ______________ .

My pet is brown and white. It's very small.
It's a ______________ .

My pet is brown. It says "bow-wow".
It's a ______________ .

My pet is black and white. It likes apples.
It's a ______________ .

My pet is green. It has got short legs.
It's a ______________ .

My pet is white. It has got long ears.
It's a ______________ .

2. Find the pets and colour the fields green. What can you see?

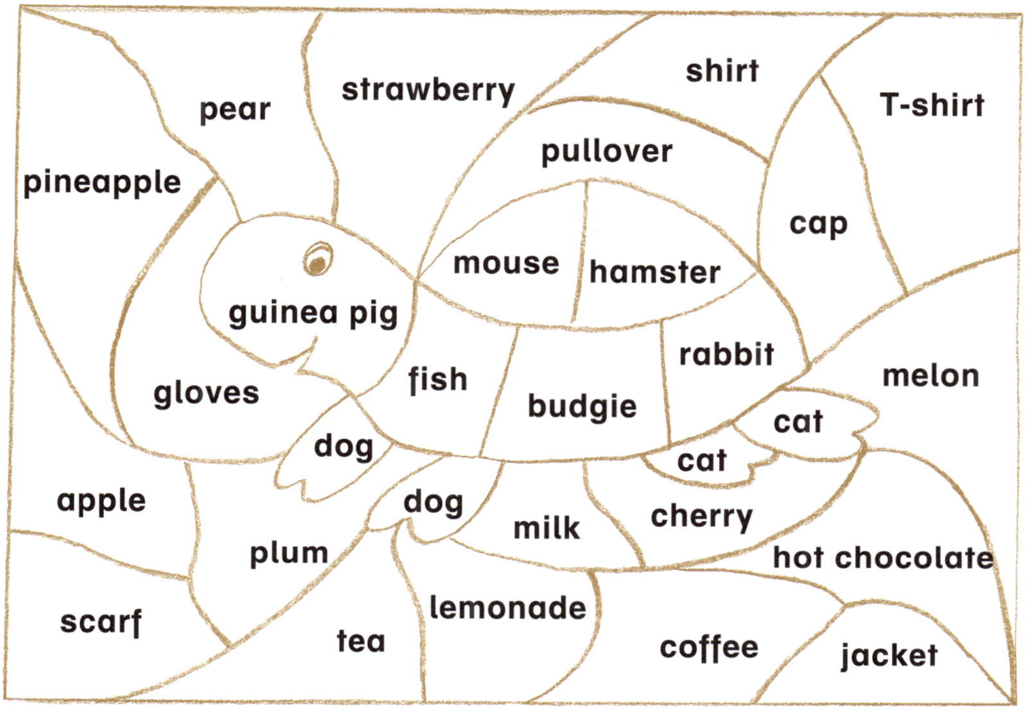

I can see a ______________________ .

3. Guess the pets. Write.

____

4. Trace the lines and write.

A ______________________ likes  .

A ______________________ likes  .

A ______________________________________  .

______________________________________  .

______________________________________  .

mouse
cat
guinea pig
dog
rabbit

1. Write and draw lines.

spring	**summer**
autumn	**winter**

Schreibe zuerst unter jedes Bild die passende Jahreszeit. Ordne dann den Jahreszeiten die Monate zu.

June

May

August

April

July

March

It's ______________ .

It's ______________ .

September

January

November

October

February

December

It's ______________ .

It's ______________ .

2. Write the 12 months in the correct order.

1. ______________ 2. ______________ 3. ______________

4. ______________ 5. ______________ 6. ______________

7. ______________ 8. ______________ 9. ______________

10. ______________ 11. ______________ 12. ______________

3. Read and tick the correct answer.

Easter is in ...

◯ winter ◯ summer ◯ spring.

Christmas is in ...

◯ December ◯ November ◯ September.

Halloween is in ...

◯ April ◯ October ◯ February.

The summer holidays are in ...

◯ January ◯ March ◯ July/August.

4. What can you see? Write.

MEV Verlag/Martin Muth

I can see a ______________ .

MEV Verlag/Waltraud Bäuerle

I can see a ______________ .

Project Photos

I can see a ______________ .

Österreich Werbung/G. Popp

I can see a ______________ .

Project Photos

I can see ______________ .

Shotshop.com/Christa Eder

I can see a ______________ .

pond

butter-fly

tree

grass

frog

flower

5. Find the months. Draw lines and write.

Octo- Novem-

Jul-

Janua-

Mar- **-ber**

Decem-

Septem-

6. What can you see?
Colour the spring words green, the summer words yellow, the autumn words brown and the winter words blue.

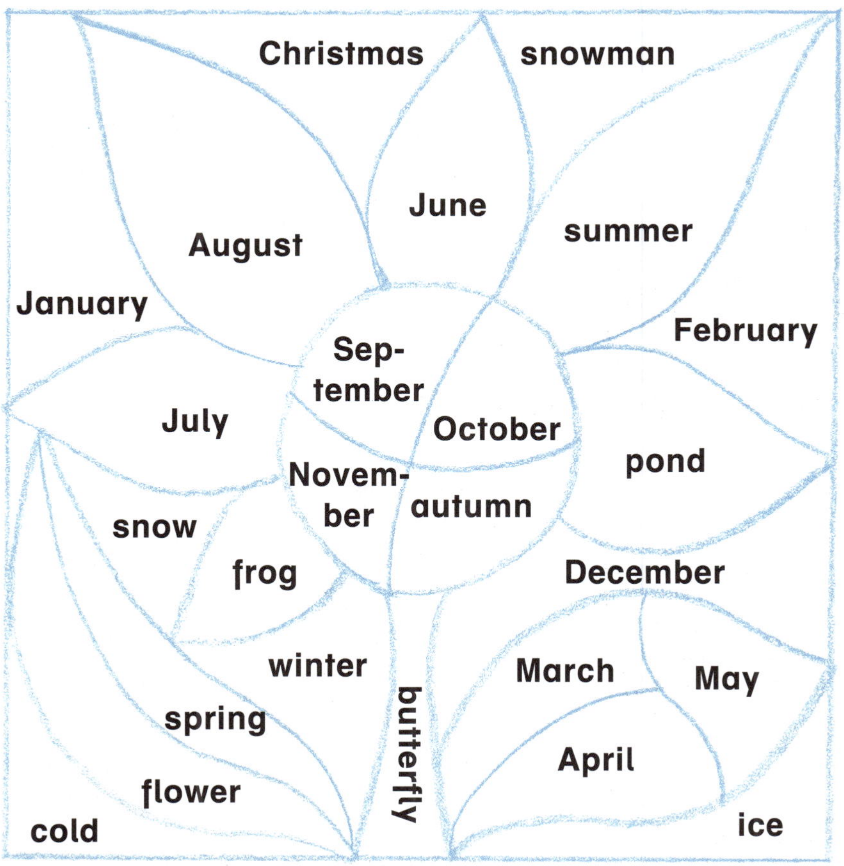

I can see a ______________________ .

1. Read the comic.

Sally in London

2. Colour the British flag – The Union Jack.

3. What can you see in the pictures? Write.

ingimage.com

VERITAS-VERLAG, Linz/Susanne Suk

ingimage.com

MEV Verlag/Paul Welt

Buckingham Palace **Tower Bridge** **London Eye** **Big Ben**

Für weitere Informationen steht Ihnen gerne Ihre VERITAS-Kundenberatung zur Verfügung.
Rufen Sie einfach an, schicken Sie ein Fax oder ein E-Mail!
Tel. 0043/(0)732/776451/2280, Fax: 0043/(0)732/776451/2239
E-Mail: kundenberatung@veritas.at
Besuchen Sie uns auf unserer Website www.veritas.at

Originaltitel: Englisch Stars 3
Erarbeitet von: Barbara Gleich, Irene Reindl, Katrin Schmidt, Britta Schöpe

8. Auflage 2022

Auf umweltfreundlichem Papier gedruckt bei: siehe https://produkt.veritas.at/29547#additional
Lektorat: Kerstin Kauffold, Geraldine Tahmassebi
Bildredaktion: Nina Autengruber
Herstellung, Umschlaggestaltung und Layout: Irene Demelmair, Jutta Creutzburg
Illustrationen: Martina Mair, Wilfried Poll
Umschlagbild: Christine Brand
Umschlagfoto: ms.foto.group / Linz
Satz: dtp Veritas, Linz

ISBN 978-3-7058-9138-8